Guess Who
Swoops

Adivina quién
baja en picada

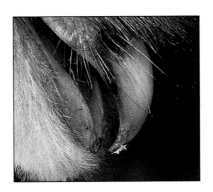

Sharon Gordon

 **Marshall Cavendish**
Benchmark
New York

Look up!

Can you see me?

I live in this big, old barn.

¡Mira arriba!

¿Me ves?

Vivo en un granero viejo
y grande.

No one knows I am here.

I hide my nest and eggs.

❖

Nadie sabe que estoy aquí,
escondiendo mi nido y
mis huevos.

I am *nocturnal*.

I get up when the sun goes down.

Soy *nocturna*.

Cuando el sol se acuesta, yo me levanto.

That is when I hunt for food.

I eat rats, mice, and small birds.

Es entonces que salgo a cazar mi comida.

Como ratas, ratones y pájaros pequeños.

My sharp claws can catch
them.

Puedo atraparlos con mis
garras filosas.

My strong beak can carry them away.

Puedo llevármelos lejos con mi fuerte pico.

I see in the dark with these small eyes.

Puedo ver en la oscuridad con estos ojos pequeños.

My hearing is the best.

I can hear a mouse far, far away.

---❖---

Mi oído es de lo mejor.

Puedo oír un ratón desde muy lejos.

I have strong wings.

I can fly quickly.

I can fly quietly.

Tengo alas muy fuertes.

Puedo volar rápida y
silenciosamente.

I swoop down.

I surprise the mouse.

❖

Yo bajo en picada y
sorprendo al ratón.

Sometimes, the mouse surprises me!

Screech!

¡A veces, el ratón me sorprende a mí!

¡Guííiiiii!

That is all right.

I have all night!

Who am I?

---❖---

No importa.

¡Tengo toda la noche!

¿Quién soy?

I am an owl!

¡Soy una lechuza!

Who am I?

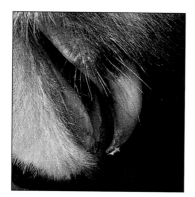

beak
pico

claws
garras

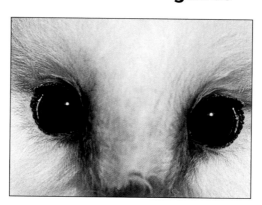

eyes
ojos

wings
alas

Challenge Words

nocturnal A word used to describe an animal that comes out at night.

Palabras avanzadas

nocturno(a) Palabra que describe a un animal que sale por la noche.

Index

Índice

About the Author
Datos biográficos de la autora

Sharon Gordon has written many books for young children. She has always worked as an editor. Sharon and her husband Bruce have three children, Douglas, Katie, and Laura, and one spoiled pooch, Samantha. They live in Midland Park, New Jersey.

❖

Sharon Gordon ha escrito muchos libros para niños. Siempre ha trabajado como editora. Sharon y su esposo Bruce tienen tres niños, Douglas, Katie y Laura, y una perra consentida, Samantha. Viven en Midland Park, Nueva Jersey.

With thanks to Nanci Vargus, Ed.D. and
Beth Walker Gambro, reading consultants

Marshall Cavendish Benchmark
99 White Plains Road
Tarrytown, New York 10591-9001
www.marshallcavendish.us

Library of Congress Cataloging-in-Publication Data

Gordon, Sharon.
[Guess who swoops. Spanish & English]
Guess who swoops = Adivina quién baja en picada / Sharon Gordon. — Bilingual ed.
p. cm. — (Bookworms. Guess who? = Adivina quién)
Includes index.
ISBN-13: 978-0-7614-2468-0 (bilingual edition)
ISBN-10: 0-7614-2468-7 (bilingual edition)
ISBN-13: 978-0-7614-2387-4 (Spanish edition)
ISBN-10: 0-7614-1553-X (English edition)
1. Owls—Juvenile literature. I. Title. II. Title: Adivina quién baja en picada. III. Series: Gordon, Sharon. Bookworms.
Guess who? (Spanish & English)

QL696.S8G6718 2006b
598.9'7—dc22
2006016817

Spanish Translation and Text Composition by Victory Productions, Inc.
www.victoryprd.com

Photo Research by Anne Burns Images

Cover Photo by: *Animals, Animals*/Richard Day

The photographs in this book are used with permission and through the courtesy of: *Animals, Animals*:
p. 3 Michael Gadomski; p. 7 Scott W. Smith; pp. 11, 28 (top right) Stephen Dalton; p. 17 Gerard Lacz.
Visuals Unlimited: p. 5 Deneve Feigh Bunde; pp. 25, 27 Joe McDonald. *Peter Arnold*: pp. 1, 13, 15, 28
(top left and bottom) Don Riepe; pp. 19, 23, 29 Gerard Lacz; p. 21 Manfred Danegger. *Corbis*: p. 9 George Lepp.

Series design by Becky Terhune

Printed in Malaysia
1 3 5 6 4 2